Old DUNOON and COWAL

by
John Macleay

According to Duncan Graham, author of *Sunset on the Clyde*, Tighnabruaich's pier was the 'core of [the community's] life and being'. Steaming away from it into the Kyles of Bute is the *King Edward*. Built in 1901 at Denny's yard in Dumbarton, this was the first commercial turbine-powered passenger steamer. It covered the Greenock–Dunoon–Rothesay–Campbeltown run and was broken up in 1928.

FURTHER READING

The books listed below are some of those used by the author during his research. None of them are available from Stenlake Publishing. Those interested in finding out more are advised to contact their local bookshop or reference library.

J.J. Bell, *Scotland's Rainbow West*, George G. Harrap and Co.

J.J. Bell, *The Glory of Scotland*, George G. Harrap and Co.

Stuart Donald, *In the Wake of the Vital Spark*, Neil Wilson Publishing.

Duncan Graham, *Sunset on the Clyde*, Neil Wilson Publishing.

E. & R. Inglis, *Dunoon and District Guide*, Dunoon.

Iain McRorie, *The Clyde Piers*, Inverclyde Libraries.

Nigel Tranter, *Argyll and Bute* (the Queen's Scotland series), Hodder and Stoughton.

ACKNOWLEDGEMENTS

The author wishes to thank the following for their invaluable help: Robert Reid, piermaster at Dunoon, and all his friendly crew; Dan Mackinlay; Kevin MacDonald; John McCormack; Roddy Black; the staff of the *Dunoon Observer*; the staff of *Dunoon Library*; Les Kerr; John Stirling and the Castle Museum, Dunoon.

Text © John Macleay, 2002.
First published in the United Kingdom, 2002,
reprinted 2006, 2010, 2011, 2013
by Stenlake Publishing Ltd,
01290 551122
www.stenlake.co.uk

ISBN 9781840332223

INTRODUCTION

The finest walk in these islands, declared a Professor Blackie, is from Gourock to the Cloch lighthouse, while the second finest is from the Cloch back to Gourock. Well, by whichever direction and whatever the weather, there is no questioning the sheer splendour and allure of those Cowal hills across the waters. Formed like some gnarled hand flexed to crush the isle of Bute, Cowal is that bunched land mass of Argyll between Loch Fyne and the inner Firth Of Clyde. It's a country of knobbly hills – mountains in contour and character – riven with weed-fringed sea lochs that merge with stream, 'wood, and rifted rock'; and though heavily timbered, this corner of the county has spots suggesting that the last Ice Age might have occurred within living memory.

Dunoon and Cowal form an inseparable, yet incongruous, pairing, for Argyll's largest centre of population is in many ways a lowland resort that has clawed a hold on the county's coastal fringe. It has been argued that the town is 'in Argyll, but not of it', but this makes for a pleasing contrast rather than clash, and makes Dunoon perfectly sited to enjoy that contrast. Mere minutes from the town there is 'music in the wild cascade' as streams surge through mossy glens, 'roarin' to the sea'; and from its busiest thoroughfare there are enticing glimpses of the hills and several handy escape routes to them. Ten minutes away, the walker can pick up a forest trail and begin seeking the hill route to roadless Loch Striven.

Through recent fluctuations of fortune and 'changes of hat', a resort Dunoon has doggedly remained. Throughout the early 1940s, with rationing and blackout regulations, the holiday trade and the war effort rubbed amicably along, and in the post-war years there was another boom with Maw, Paw and the weans annually going 'doon the watter'. In the 'big weeks' the town could seem like an outpost of Glasgow (arguably its development came about as such), yet by the late 1950s and early '60s there was talk of the 'Costas' rather than Colintraive or Cairndow and the disquieting news of pier closures. Annually there were fewer of those familiar yellow-and-black funnelled steamers, every other one seemingly named after a Walter Scott novel or one of its characters – *Talisman, Jeannie Deans, Lucy Ashton, Waverley* – and then, in the early 1960s, came the 'friendly occupation' of the US Navy which lasted until the 1990s.

These waves and troughs have inevitably wrought changes, but Dunoon, as well as clinging to its sense of purpose, has kept its own genial identity and has managed to avoid the run-down seediness of a holiday town in decline; and anyway, without ever being aloof, it never quite went in for Blackpool brashness or raucous leisure, although anyone who has witnessed the 'parade of the thousand pipers' finale to the August Highland Gathering will realise that it *can* be good-naturedly uninhibited.

For many who have been long familiar with the district, Dunoon – and a couple of miles of shoreline either side – is Cowal, *their* Cowal, and they have never seen cause to venture into the hill and forest of Glen Kin or looked on the stream in Glen Massan when it is 'big wi' spate'. There are those regularly holidaying, or even living, in Tighnabruaich who will never have searched for the alleged 'path' skirting Loch Riddon, or entered the woods where ferns and ivy have reclaimed the ruins of the gunpowder industry. The angler who for years has 'flogged' Loch Eck may know nothing of the Paper Cave concealed on the hillside above (this is a cavern 500 feet above the shore which was used as a hiding place for the Clan Campbell's documents and deeds). But this hardly matters, for they are fully appreciating their own Cowal.

Cowal is the part of the West Highlands closest to Glasgow, yet it remains, in parts, as remote as districts further west or north, some stretches of its probing sea lochs being devoid of roads and giving this region the fascination of being at once familiar, yet largely unknown. From his birthplace across Loch Fyne, Neil Munro looked daily on Cowal's hills and he might have been speaking of them when he favoured 'a stance inland from the salt water, where the mountain air, brushing over gall and heather, takes the sting from the sea air, and the two blended give a notion of the fine variousness of life.' Cowal offers many such stances and there is some of that variousness in this book's sometimes unfamiliar views of well-known, much loved – and in some cases sorely-missed – landmarks, all of them part of somebody's Cowal.

Opposite: Cairndow, near the head of Loch Fyne, is properly pronounced *cairn dhu* which might be an allusion to the dark hill seen here behind Ardkinglas House. According to Para Handy, Cairndow is where they 'keep the two New Years', a reference to the alteration in the calender in 1752 when there was anxiety among the dwellers along Loch Fyne over which was the correct date on which to observe the festivities; they solved the problem by celebrating on both possible occasions! The house was built by Robert Lorimer in 1907 and looks much the same today. The Strone Gardens nearby are worth seeing, especially for the 188 foot Douglas fir.

A 1909 view of Dunoon's pier with its distinctive Tudor design. Despite changes and upgradings throughout the twentieth century, it is recognisably the same, although the promenade deck on the right is no longer a feature. This was a seating area, convenient for watching for arrivals, and just as handy for passing an entire day, whether watching the cut-throat competition between steamers racing for the pier or the shipping – puffers, paddlers, or 'yatts' – slipping in and out of the Clyde. Throughout the Second World War many of these craft were grey, part of the legendary North Atlantic convoys. In the same era the Sunderland flying boats, berthed in the Gareloch, skimmed these waters. There had been landing stages for centuries at this obvious crossing point, but the first pier was built in 1835, later to be improved by the Stevenson brothers (one of whom was the father of Robert Louis Stevenson). The present structure dates from 1898. Cars were still a novelty in 1909 (so much so that the postcard manufacturer appears to have superimposed them onto this shot!), but later they brought an end to the steamers in favour of vehicle ferries. Mainly used today by Caledonian MacBrayne ferries, the pier is still visited by the *Waverley*, 'the world's last seagoing paddle steamer'.

The black discs on the tower of Dunoon's pier indicated which berths were available to approaching steamers (reversible, they were white on the back). Though this signalling system (their invention was the outcome of a competition) is long disused, the apparatus is still maintained. In the inter-war years a loudspeaker system was installed, but as this was also used to play music, it caused some distress among some hard line Sabbatarians. While J.J. Bell allowed that Dunoon did not 'discourage the louder gaieties', this was never the brash leisure complex that English piers sought to be. There was a tea room/café and also slot machines, one of which needed a penny to allow you to 'make your own nameplate' on a hopelessly flexible metal strip. In more recent times some of the buildings have been used as entertainment venues. This view also shows on the right mile-distant Kirn pier and the Dunbartonshire shore at the mouth of Loch Long.

Opened in 1905, the Pavilion at Dunoon was used as a dance hall and also hosted what the comedian Denny Willis styled as 'Cowal Carnival' type shows which, while aimed at a Glasgow audience, endeavoured to provide a local flavour with songs, scenes and sketches about the area. Before burning down in 1958, the venue also featured 'big names' from radio and variety who were making the transition to television, including Donald Peers, Issy Bonn, Freddie Sales, and Billy Stutt. During the First World War religious services were held here for the troops and the legendary Highland Light Infantry were actually billeted on the premises. Catholic services were also held here prior to the opening of the Brandon Street R.C. church. While the design was generally praised, it was lamented that its lines were marred by later building in the immediate vicinity. It was replaced in the early 1960s by the Queen's Hall. For obvious reasons the Argyll Hotel (still in business) was probably more popular than the Temperance Hotel facing it across the street. In the early nineteenth century one of the town's attractions was the opportunity to drink goats' whey for health reasons (goats were easier to keep than cattle and occasionally there was a surplus of goats' milk).

The gas lamps on Dunoon's Esplanade are long gone and the gardens are laid out differently today; but the bandstand is still there, as well as the weighbridge building at the entrance to the coal pier where cargo-carrying carts or lorries were weighed when moving on or off the ferries. The similar crow-stepped building across the road, in the centre of the picture, functioned as a café but was cleared to make way for extensions to the Argyll Hotel. Ben More and the Kilmun Hills are in the extreme distance, while the high ground to the right of the hospital's chimney (centre background) is the site of the local golf course. The clock tower to left of the hospital chimney belongs to the convalescent homes, but both of these institutions have since been demolished. In the days when this photograph was taken, the second Saturday in August would see this area thronged with spectators of the annual swim from Dunoon to the Cloch, but this was discontinued in the mid-1950s.

Even in Argyll Street, Dunoon's busiest thoroughfare, it's hard to remain unaware of the hills, although recent afforestation has smothered the contours of the Dunan. While there are no traffic jams, the garage and 'motor tours' signs indicate that the car is catching on. The buildings beyond the distinctive cinema on the left (The Picture House, built in 1913) are of St Cuthbert's Church, now demolished. Argyll Street is the setting for the stunning 'parade of the thousand pipers', the grand finale to the Cowal Highland Gathering which occurs every last Saturday in August.

With a Queen Street, Clyde Street, Argyll Street and Alexandra Parade, it's small wonder that Glaswegians feel at home in Dunoon. This is possibly why, in a coastal town, it was deemed necessary to advertise a 'Glasgow Restaurant'. Another cinema, the La Scala, opened in this street in 1931.

This post office, at the northern end of Argyll Street, opened in 1902. A tenement known as the 'Commercial Buildings' and bearing the date 1910 now occupies the walled, railed space facing it, dating this picture to the very earliest years of the twentieth century. Beyond the trees are the burgh buildings and the now demolished St Cuthbert's.

When this photograph was taken, this part of the upper reaches of Argyll Street was known as Manse Road. Beyond the trees and the white houses stand the convalescent homes, although by 1910 this view would have been somewhat obscured by the tenement erected at the end of this parade where the low wall is, opposite the Post Office.

In 1869 the Glasgow and West of Scotland Convalescent Homes at Dunoon were inaugurated by a Miss Beatrice Clugston and, fitted out with '330 beds and cribs', were intended in 'assisting, by a generous dietary and a bracing and restful atmosphere, in the recovery of those laid aside by illness'. For the best part of a century it afforded welcome breaks for many convalescing Glasgow folk sorely in need of them, before eventual demolition in 1973. The modern library stands in the parkland which the buildings occupied and the nearby rose garden in John Street was once the Homes' own bowling green. Not many of those using the homes would utilise cabs or taxis, but they would willingly part with two or three pence to have their bags or cases carried from the pier. 'A tanner was exceptional', recalled Dan Mackinlay who lugged many a case along that route. During the Second World War, the Homes became HMS *Osprey*, an establishment specialising in 'degaussing' (the process of proofing ships' magnetic fields against mines).

Mere minutes from busy Argyll Street, this site is today a secluded and even leafier spot, although it still allows terrific views towards the Clyde, Loch Long and the Rosneath Peninsula. Designed by Gillespie Graham, the Parish Church was completed in 1816 on a site long dedicated to church and chapel. There are some seventeenth century graves, some carvings that previously were in St Cuthbert's, and – for the grisly-minded – a circular watch house from the days of the 'resurrectionists', a facetious name for the 'sack-em-up-boys' or, more simply, the body-snatchers.

Although both Arran and Kintyre have claimed Mary Campbell as a native (her given name was Margaret), she was born in 1766 at Achamore (which translates as 'Big Field') Farm, Dunoon. In Ayr, where she met Robert Burns, her accent singled her out as 'Highland Mary'. Her statue was erected on Castle Hill in 1896, the centenary of Burns's death, and the bible which she clutches represents the one used in their irregular (but seemingly not illegal) marriage ceremony. Burns mentioned her in several of his verses and apparently they planned to emigrate to the West Indies together. However, she died in Greenock in 1786, possibly during a typhus epidemic, although some of the poet's biographers have controversially claimed that it was more likely she was pregnant by him and both she and the child died during its birth. No longer a working farm, the yard and byre are presently being used by a haulage firm.

This view of the beach at Victoria Parade shows just what a popular business boat-hiring was in the 1920s. Even in the late 1950s there were some twenty hirers in business at Dunoon, most based here on the West Bay, although Alex Waddell ran fishing trips, a Kilmun ferry service, and rowing boat hire on Holy Loch, while Archie Sands had a 'guid-gaun business' at Port Riddell on the East Bay.

Extensive storm damage at the West Bay, pictured in 1916. According to Peter, the sender of this card (who was presumably very young!), it put the beach out of bounds for 'playing shops'. The wreckage here is mainly of garden walls, although the basements suffered flooding. The building crowned by ironwork is now the Milton Tower Hotel, a few minutes stroll from the pier.

While this car is custom-built, there is no information about either the builder or owner. It has been suggested that it belonged to Sir Harry Lauder as he had two homes locally, but would he have been so publicity shy not appear in the photograph? Another possibility is that it belonged to 'Uncle Dick' Southerd, named on the playbill for Dunoon's 'Cosy Corner'. This building is definitely not the 'Corner', a tin-roofed, earthen-floored, seafront theatre where some big names appeared, including Jack Buchanan, Tommy Lorne, the Tiller Girls, Harry Gordon, Alec Finlay, and George West. It stood until 1960 and eight years later the swimming pool was built on its site.

Possibly dating from 1878, this is certainly the oldest card in this collection and Kirn appears to be little more than a street, although the queue of vehicles suggest that the pier was doing brisk business. The distant houses mark where the church now stands and some of the nearer buildings were probably cleared to create space for the Esplanade. There is no evidence of Kirn as a place-name prior to the 1700s and it may take its name from the 'churns' or millstones which were fashioned here from local stone. The quarries can still be found on the high ground behind the village and by Loch Loskin.

Although Kirn pier wasn't especially large it boasted some conspicuous, even garish, buildings ('like a small version of the Kremlin' ran a local joke) so that it could easily be picked out from the 'Gourock side' of the Firth. Just beyond the buildings was the approach to the jetty, now derelict, and there is little trace of the pier itself which operated from 1845 and closed down in the 1960s. The weighing machine to the right of its entrance was still there in the 1950s. The ornate structure on the left is the currently closed Queen's Hotel.

Taken from Kirn pier, this photograph shows in the foreground the jetty which was a coal pier and calling point for the 'puffers' that moored and unloaded here throughout the 1950s. It was also popular with generations of youngsters who learned here about catching fish (or how to fib about those nearly landed). A passenger ferry to the Cloch lighthouse also operated from here. Now in poor repair, it is no longer even visible, let alone accessible, from the street thanks to some recent building.

Kirn Brae, pictured around 1909. The red sandstone church was completed not long before, the stone having been quarried in Corrie on the isle of Arran. The houses in front of the tower were cleared away, presumably to allow easier access to traffic turning up Kirn Brae, and the church is now fronted by a lawn. The buildings opposite are still there, although the post office is now sited on the esplanade.

In this view of the Esplanade at Kirn the Kilmun hills and Strone Point are plainly visible with, just by the hut, a large yacht slipping out of Holy Loch. The picture dates from before the First World War when the wooded ground immediately beyond was apparently still clear of development. Although it's hard to find among the rocks now, there was a sizeable paddling pool that on wild days could be positively dangerous to non-swimmers when waves broke over it, making it far deeper than any paddling pool should be.

Described on the back of the photograph as simply an 'inhabitant' of Kirn Gardens, it's not clear whether this man was a holidaymaker, member of staff or an entertainer hired to heighten the international atmosphere.

Any level, leafy ground in Kirn has to be near the water's edge, but it's difficult to reconcile this setting, named as the Café Chantant, with the 'Kirn Gardens' on today's seafront. It has been suggested that the gardens shown here were actually in Clyde Street on the Dunoon side of Kirn pier. Whatever the case, this looks like a wholehearted enterprise, for while the name has a French ambiance, the other picture shows Chinese lettering on one of the buildings so perhaps there was an attempt to capture not just a continental effect, but a truly international one. While there is some uncertainty as to the precise location, some of today's locals have 'heard tell of it' and apparently among the entertainments featured were 'minstrel shows'.

Hunter's Quay was named after the age-of-steam entrepreneur James Hunter of Hafton and his name replaced the more evocative *Camusreannach* ('Bay of Ferns'). The magnificent Royal Marine Hotel overlooks the quay. It had its own tiny post office (now a coffee shop) close by, originally built as a telegraph office for receiving news of the various yacht races. Also serving as the base of the Royal Clyde Yacht Club, the hotel remains a reminder of the great 'Clyde Fortnight' of regattas which were held until the nuclear submarine base on Holy Loch inhibited such activities.

Standing at the entrance to Holy Loch, the pier at Hunter's Quay is possibly the most attractive on the Clyde. In 1858 the pile-supported extension was added to the original stone quay which had been completed in 1829. Extensively used for almost a hundred years, it was under threat of closure by 1951, a poor reward for its service as Dunoon's pier during wartime blackout hours. However, it didn't actually close until 1964 and Western Ferries bought it five years later, launching in 1973 the crossing from MacInroy's Point, south of Gourock. While this service is still going, sadly the variety of craft seen here no longer calls.

The *Marchioness of Lorne* steaming into Ardnadam pier which, at some 200 feet, is the longest of the upper Clyde piers. Holy Loch was famed already for yacht building – producing such Americas Cup challengers as *Sovereign* and *Sceptre* and servicing Sir Tommy Lipton's *Shamrock* – so there were already slips and jetties at Robertson's and Morris & Lorrimer's yards, but nothing big enough to accommodate passenger vessels. Built in 1858, this pier came to be used as an overnight berth for the Craigendoran steamers, but by 1939 only one vessel called regularly and it closed to commercial traffic the following year. The years of the Second World War saw it taken over (along with nearby Ardnadam Hotel) by the Admiralty and then by the US Navy. Due to anti-nuclear protests in the early 1960s, this pier became familiar in television news broadcasts. It still stands and is just as long, although it has been stripped of its 'shipping boxes' and signalling equipment.

'Oor wee schule's a nice wee schule . . . ' ran an old song, the sentiments of which would seem to shared by these pupils of the school at Sandbank. Understandable, too, in such a beautiful setting, but what was the occasion that had to be captured on camera? Was it a school outing, a celebration, or just the school 'photie'? The year is difficult to ascertain, but it was probably taken before the First World War. Dan MacKinlay, who spent much of the inter-war years as a boy hereabouts, told me that his mother attended this school as far back as 1889 and it served Sandbank until the 1970s when the new school on the 'High Road' opened. It is now a community centre. The sandbank after which the village is named is the tidal flats where the Big and Little Echaigs flow into the loch and where the lighters called to take on gunpowder from the mills at Clachaig.

Is Sandbank's Ferguslie Road named after the area in Paisley with the same name? Certainly the Coats and other Paisley families in the thread industry had their residences and boats here on Holy Loch, and back around 1807 Whitefarland Point was renamed Lazaretto Point when it became a quarantine station where raw cotton bales were 'purified' before going on to Paisley's Ferguslie Mills for processing. (A lazaretto was a dwelling for lepers and while there was no actual threat of leprosy here, cotton can nonetheless carry other germs or 'plagues' and it was stored here in the open for a period of quarantine before being sent on to mills in Paisley and Glasgow.) The once thriving yacht yards sustained several suppliers and chandlers' stores like the one pictured.

Ben More simply means 'big hill' and the one on Loch Eck side gives its name to this estate and house, built by James Duncan, a sugar refiner and early conservationist. He began a systematic tree-planting programme here around 1870. A later proprietor, Harry George Younger, whose product is still enjoyed in pubs throughout the land, presented the

10,200 acre estate to the nation in 1928 and it has since been used as a base for training forestry personnel and as an outdoor centre. Among the guests who were invited to this striking residence were Henry Morton Stanley, remembered for his 'presumptuous' greeting to the explorer, David Livingston, and Spurgeon the Baptist evangelist who preached here to a crowd of 7,000. Unfortunately the magnificent glass houses in the gardens failed to survive a storm in the 1920s and part of their site is taken by the memorial hut – previously in Puck's Glen – to Balfour Bailley, the eminent botanist.

Throughout Argyll there are wells and the remains of shrines and chapels dedicated to St Catherine; veneration of her may have already been centuries old when, in 1450, Duncan, first Lord Campbell, built the church of St Catherine's and gave this neighbourhood its name. Facing Inverary across Loch Fyne, this ideally located hostelry, long known to anglers, soon became as popular with the passing trade from motorists which was just beginning when this photograph was taken in 1922. In earlier times the inns at this spot would have been well patronised by the drovers whose cattle were ferried across the loch at this point.

A view from the old pier at Strachur, the most populous community along Loch Fyne's eastern shore. It once claimed to be Cowal's 'capital' and certainly it was noted for its cattle fairs. Happily, there are few changes to this scene, near which lived Labour Party leader John Smith, and still more recently you could have been served a drink by 'the real James Bond', Sir Fitzroy MacLean. A distinguished diplomat, adventurer, author and soldier, he was the basis for Fleming's hero and in his later years kept the Creggans Inn just north of here and also owned the old MacArthur estate.

Loch Eck was a great favourite with English visitors and not just because they could pronounce it. Whether its seven-mile length was covered by foot, horse, or boat, it provided a quick route to the lowland shores, as well as being a funeral route for those Campbells of Argyll interred at Kilmun. In the nineteenth century an iron steamship ploughed its waters, and there was a later vessel called *Fairy Queen*, but such delightful travel was killed off by the advent of the motor coach. These passengers, pictured around 1906, were probably heading off to undertake such a sail. It was possible to take ship from Glasgow to the Holy Loch, transfer to a coach to the foot of Loch Eck, embark again to meet another coach from the top of the loch to Strachur, and then take the ferry across Loch Fyne to Inverary.

Strachur pier closed in 1935, although it was reported to be in dangerously poor repair a decade earlier. There had been a pier of sorts here for centuries and Mary, Queen of Scots, once stepped ashore here after a crossing from Inverary. Other visitors have included Keats, Wordsworth and Chopin.

The wooded surroundings soften the 'company town' look of these houses at Millhouse, most of which owe their existence to the gunpowder mills that operated hereabouts between 1839 and 1921. The remains of these can be found along the stream and among the trees. There was already a tradition of gunpowder production in Cowal (probably due to the wealth of suitable timber for making charcoal), there having been manufacture in Glen Lean back in the Napoleonic era. These works, at one time owned by the Kames Gunpowder Company, were important enough to justify a military presence at times. In the aftermath of the First World War, author Ratcliffe Barnett, observed making notes and consulting a map, was reported by overzealous locals as a spy. His brief predicament was doubly embarrassing as he was also a clergyman.

Today Millhouse's gunpowder mills would probably be preserved as industrial archaeology, but if locally they weren't sick of the sight of them, people as far away as Rothesay, Dunoon and Inverary were certainly sick of their sound, there having been some half a dozen explosions over the eighty odd years of production. By a cottage at the edge of the village hangs the bell that once summoned the workers, but now it only rings to welcome in the New Year. On a board beneath it are the names of those who lost their lives in the various blasts.

Kames derives from the Gaelic *camus* ('a bay'), the original name being *Camus Na Mucklach* or 'bay of the pigsties'. Some of these houses were erected prior to the First World War for the managerial staff of the gunpowder mills. Most of the powder was manufactured at Millhouse, but there was, as this card shows, a small industrial complex around the pier, as well as storage facilities. Most of that has been cleared from the pierhead area, but curiously the low, makeshift boathouses verging on the shore (behind the beached rowing boat) are still there today, contradicting a well-known assertion that the local midges can 'bite their way through corrugated iron roofs'.

'It would be vain to pretend,' J.J. Bell argued, 'that Kames was ever Tighnabruaich's pretty sister', but this obviously contented group shows little concern with such criticism or comparison. Gone now are the squat chimney and 'industrial intrusions', and the only trade carried on around the pierhead now is that of the local coal merchant.

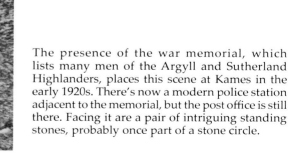

The presence of the war memorial, which lists many men of the Argyll and Sutherland Highlanders, places this scene at Kames in the early 1920s. There's now a modern police station adjacent to the memorial, but the post office is still there. Facing it are a pair of intriguing standing stones, probably once part of a stone circle.

In this view Kames pier has not yet acquired the unsightly cluster of buildings evident in other photographs. It was here that some of the ingredients vital to gunpowder production were delivered, the finished product being shipped out again after being hauled on horse-drawn vehicles from the mills. It's unlikely, though, that such a cargo would go on board the *Lord of the Isles* which, as can be seen, often carried a hefty complement of passengers. The second vessel to carry that name, she was built in Glasgow in 1891 and by 1912 was doing a daily sail around the isle of Bute. Beyond is the northern tip of Bute and the mouth of Loch Riddon.

Kames and Tighnabruaich viewed from Kames Farm. This is probably an outbuilding rather than the farm itself, which stands hard by one of Cowal's hillside golf courses and overlooks the road which linked Kames with the powder mills at Millhouse. Tranquil it may look, but the concentration of explosives produced, stored and transported couldn't have made for a relaxing atmosphere. One explosion hurled a half-ton gear wheel over a distance of two miles.

The post office at Tighnabruaich is now a few doors along and the scrub in the left foreground was cleared long ago.

There has been a bit of widening to the gate in front of the church at Tighnabruaich, presumably for car access, and there is no longer a weather vane on the bell tower. A few more tree plantations might have softened the outlines of the hills here and there, but this remains as enchanting a spot as it was when this photograph was taken.

This concrete enclosure at Tighnabruaich's East Bay seems to be a seating area and sandpit, but some insist that it was, or at least contained, a paddling pool. The distant buildings in the far right belong to the boat yard at Port Driseach, where the path can be picked up along Loch Riddon (which is alternatively known as Loch Ruel).

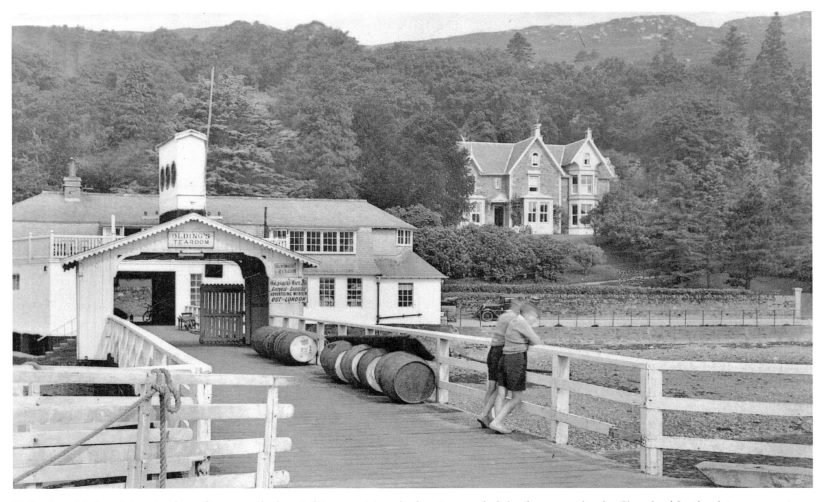

Tighnabruaich translates simply as 'house on the brae'; this one, pictured when it was a holiday home run by the Church of Scotland, is now a private dwelling. On the pier the gate house bearing the signalling tower is gone, but the balcony remains in place and even if there's not much large shipping today the pier gives a marvellous view across the narrow kyles to Bute. There has been talk of closure, but there is at present a campaign to save this unobtrusive but distinctive structure.

Built in 1864, PS *Iona* – pictured here at Tighnabruaich – was still in service in the 1930s when J.J. Bell confirmed that time had 'taken nothing from her, in fine appearance, equipment and speed'. At that time she did the run from Fort William to Oban.

Blackfarland is on the rugged, roadless north-west quarter of Bute, almost facing Tighnabruaich across the kyles. These are scenically stunning sailing waters, unarguably the 'yachtsman's paradise' that the brochures claim and just as popular today. There are several sailing schools in the area and there's still a boat-building yard at Port Driseach (which possibly translates as 'port of the briars').

Now that the clachan of Glendaruel is 'by-passed', the houses facing the hotel have been able to acquire gardens. Until the early 1950s one of these was a smithy actually run by a man named Smith. The tree is still there and behind the hotel, on the left, are the school, Kilmodan Church, and the marvellous River Ruel which opens out into Loch Riddon.

The Hotel, Glendaruel.

Telegrams: "Hotel, Glendaruel."
Salmon and Sea Trout Fishing free to Hotel Guests.

TEA ROOM

As well as fishing rights, guests at the Glendaruel Hotel were entitled to 'electric light throughout' in a district where this wasn't generally available until the late 1940s. The generator is still there. The tearoom on the left was later replaced by a two storey extension and is still in business. While it is a tiny place, 'Clachan Glendaruel' is a well-known song and the name figures in at least three famous pipe tunes, as well as playing its part in the Celtic saga of *Deirdre of the Sorrows*.

Back in 1945 this splendid baronial bargain came on the market for a mere £10,000 and while there were attempts to raise the finance locally, it was purchased by a Glasgow family who ran it as the Highland Hotel. It had previously belonged to the Cripps family, one of whom was the surgeon who enjoyed the obscure distinction of performing the first appendicectomy on a member of the Royal Family! At the time of the sale, cabinet member Sir Stafford Cripps was about to become Chancellor of the Exchequer. A man as austere as the post-war era, he was rumoured to live only on water cress which he grew on his desk blotter. Sadly this building was destroyed by fire in 1970 and the site is now a caravan park.

The old mill at Colintraive was demolished in 1960 to make way for a community centre and village hall, although the water course and dam are still traceable. While functioning as a mill, from 1808 it also doubled as a smiddy, the bellows from which are on display inside the centre. A lintel displaying a smith's hammer, a horseshoe and the date 1808 is also incorporated into the building. This site is just beyond the hotel, a few hundred yards up from the ferry stage. The crossing to Bute from here is a mere 300 yards.

Some miles south of Innellan is the lighthouse at Toward, standing on a low lying, exposed promontory which, despite its proximity to Bute, commands a clear view down the Firth. Standing fifty-six feet above the high water mark, this light is no longer manned and there's little trace of the pier other than a stone gateway. However, the adjacent buildings are still there. The first light shone back in 1812 and by the 1850s there was a sizeable little community around it. However, this was still scarcely enough to justify the erection of the pier around 1860 and this was never fully used. After 1922 it received no regular calls, although for a time it was hoped that the (ultimately short-lived) existence of the oil drilling platform yard at nearby Ardyne would see it in use again.

None of these names now appear above these shops on Innellan's Main Street, but the place otherwise looks identical today. Just as Glasgow merchants brought about Dunoon's expansion, Greenock's entrepreneurs saw Innellan as a spot within easy commuting distance. Though virtually linked to Dunoon by a four-mile string of villas, it remained fiercely independent of its larger neighbour and even though it was only a community of a thousand it had its own gasworks, water supply and four churches. One of the ministers, the blind George Matheson who was based here between 1868 and 1886, composed in the manse the haunting hymn 'O Love That Will Not Let Me Go'. On a different musical level, the first knighted music hall star, Harry Lauder, had a home nearby (appropriately on the 'Bonnie Banks of the Clyde'), while a much earlier visitor was the nursing pioneer, Florence Nightingale.

The long, low, structure facing the pier in this view of Innellan is now a garage, while the stone building just left of the pier is a Masonic lodge and the one behind that a bar. The pier came into being in 1850 and was served by a Greenock–Rothesay run, although during both world wars, being outside of the anti-submarine boom, it was served from Wemyss Bay, three miles distant on the Renfrewshire shore. Already under threat of closure by the 1950s, its last official call was in 1972, although it briefly reopened in 1974 to transport workers to McAlpine's oil rig building yard at Ardyne on Loch Striven. Today, only the pierhead buildings remain.

'Challenging' is a term regularly applied to Cowal's golf courses which are ingeniously laid out on steep, broken ground. This nine-hole course at Innellan, close to what's left of the old Campbell stronghold of Knockamillie, is a good example and it is of some consolation that if you don't have a good game you still get a grand view, although forestry and the addition of a clubhouse have certainly changed this 1914 scene. The name Innellan derives from the Gaelic word for 'island' and may mean 'Bird Island', a reference to the Perch, a spit jutting seaward south of the old pier which is irresistible to shore birds.

While you're unlikely to meet much horse-drawn transport or coachmen in scarlet livery today, this delightful road leading south to Innellan from Bullwood is almost unchanged, although in the 1970s and '80s there was some reinforcing to cope with the heavy traffic heading for the rig-building yard at Ardyne. This has not marred the marvellous views of ships, seabirds and even seals in the Firth, as well as Dunoon which dominates the background.